A
gift
honoring
Griffin
and
Carson
Gilchrist

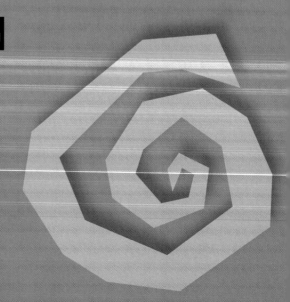

Mysterious You

Baa!

The most interesting book you'll ever read about genes and cloning

Written by Cynthia Pratt Nicolson

Illustrated by Rose Cowles

Kids Can Press

To my siblings, Derek, Shauna, Kathy and Michael
and the memory of our dad, Ken Pratt.

Two scientists gave generously of their time and expertise to help with this book. I am grateful to
Dr. Michael Smith, winner of the 1993 Nobel Prize for chemistry, who commented on the first
sections of the manuscript shortly before his untimely death in the fall of 2000. My thanks also go to
Dr. Steven Pelech of the University of British Columbia for his thorough and enthusiastic review of the
book. As well, I would like to thank Val Wyatt for her editorial support throughout this challenging
project and Rose Cowles for her zany illustrations.

Kids Can Press acknowledges the financial support of the Ontario Arts
Council, the Canada Council for the Arts and the Government of
Canada, through the BPIDP, for our publishing activity.

Published in Canada by
Kids Can Press Ltd.
29 Birch Avenue
Toronto, ON M4V 1E2

Published in the U.S. by
Kids Can Press Ltd.
2250 Military Road
Tonawanda, NY 14150

www.kidscanpress.com

Edited by Valerie Wyatt
Designed by Marie Bartholomew
Printed and bound in China

The hardcover edition of this book is smyth sewn casebound.
The paperback edition of this book is limp sewn with a drawn-on cover.

CM 01 0 9 8 7 6 5 4 3 2
CM PA 01 0 9 8 7 6 5 4 3

Canadian Cataloguing in Publication Data

Nicolson, Cynthia Pratt
    Baa! : the most interesting book you'll ever read
    about genes and cloning

(Mysterious you)
Includes index.

ISBN-13: 978-1-55074-856-7 (bound)   ISBN-10: 1-55074-856-4 (bound)
ISBN-13: 978-1-55074-886-4 (pbk.)   ISBN-10: 1-55074-886-6 (pbk.)

1. Genes — Juvenile literature. 2. Cloning — Juvenile literature.
3. Human genetics — Juvenile literature. 4. Genetics — Juvenile
literature. I. Cowles, Rose, 1967–   . II. Title. III. Series: Mysterious
you (Toronto, Ont.).

QH437.5.N52 2001   j572.8'6   C00-932961-7

Kids Can Press is a *corus*™ Entertainment company

Contents

It's in Their Genes

Robert Shafran was bewildered. The 19 year old had just arrived at college in Upper New York State and already people seemed to know him. As he walked across the campus, other students smiled, waved and even gave him hugs. What was going on?

Things began to make sense when Robert was shown a photo of a student named Eddy Galland. The smiling face staring back at Robert looked exactly like his own. Robert knew that he had been adopted as a baby. What he didn't know, until that September day, was that he had an identical twin.

When Robert and Eddy nervously met, they discovered that their resemblance went much further than their faces. Their size and body build were the same. They both had struggled with the same school subjects and done equally well in wrestling, their favorite sport. The twins' reunion was big news around the college. It was even reported in the New York City papers. But an unusual story was soon to become even more remarkable.

David Kellman, another 19 year old, was reading the newspaper when he saw the photo of Robert and Eddy. "You're not going to believe this," David told his mother as he showed her the paper. Mrs. Kellman looked at the photo — and then at her adopted son. It was like looking at the same young man copied three times. There was no doubt about it — David, Robert and Eddy were identical triplets!

Who's Who?

How could David, Robert and Eddy be alike in so many ways? It's because their genes are identical. Genes are tiny bits of matter found in every part of you. They tell your body how to function — and how to grow. Like the software running a supercomputer, your genes direct the incredibly complicated job of you being YOU.

- **Your complete set of genes is called your genome (say Jen-ome).**

- **Scientists who study genes are called geneticists.**

- **Feeling mousy? No wonder! Over 90 percent of the human genome is identical to that of a mouse. More than one-third matches the genome of the tiny nematode worm. Even so, each species of plant and animal has some genes that are unique. That's why mother mice give birth to baby mice, not baby pigs, and acorns produce oak trees, not carrots.**

Genes and More

Genes are powerful but they don't have complete control. The food you eat, the places you live and the things you do also affect the person you become. For instance, your genes might carry the instructions for building strong muscles. But what if you're a serious couch potato? Sorry — in spite of those great genes, you could still end up flabby.

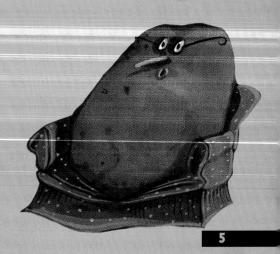

Peas Reveal Gene Secrets

Gregor Mendel was sick of peas. By 1865, the Austrian monk had grown thousands of pea plants in his monastery's garden. Mendel wasn't cooking vats of pea soup. He was using the little green vegetables to solve a scientific mystery: how do parents pass traits (special features) to their children?

Mendel began his investigations in 1856. In one series of experiments, he fertilized white-flowered peas with pollen from their red-flowered cousins. Then he planted the seeds that formed.

When the next generation of plants grew flowers, Mendel noticed that all of them were red. It seemed that only the red-flower trait was passed on—the trait of having white flowers had vanished.

Next Mendel crossed these red-flowered plants with each other. He was in for a surprise. About one-quarter of them produced plants that had white flowers. The lost trait had reappeared!

Considering the Clues

For eight long years, Mendel continued to analyze pea plants. He carefully recorded thousands of flowers, pods, seeds and stems. He discovered that parents pass on traits to their children as if each trait were carried in a separate, tiny package. He called these packages "particles of inheritance." Today we know them as genes.

Mendel realized that genes come in pairs—one from each parent. Sometimes one of these genes overpowers another. In the case of peas, the gene for red flowers overpowers the gene for white flowers. To have white flowers, a pea plant must inherit white-flower genes from both parents. Mendel called these two forms of a trait "dominant" and "recessive," words we still use today.

Gregor Mendel is called the father of genetics. In his own lifetime, however, other scientists ignored his findings. One even wrote that Mendel hadn't done enough work. The discouraged monk stopped his experiments. No more peas, please!

You Try It

Just like peas, people have dominant and recessive traits. For instance, check out your earlobes. Are they attached or dangling? The gene for free-hanging earlobes is dominant. Attached earlobes are a recessive trait. Free-hanging earlobes could mean that you have two "free-hanging" genes—or that you have a mix of free-hanging and attached genes. If you have attached earlobes, you've inherited an "attached" gene from both your parents.

free-hanging earlobe   attached earlobe

Hoop Dreams Depend on Genes

Heard of basketball superstar Michael Jordan? What about his older brother, Larry? As kids, Michael and Larry were evenly matched on the basketball court. Both were superb young athletes who could jump, shoot and dribble with dazzling skill. And both made the most of their natural talent by practicing for hours at a time. Why did only one brother become world famous? The answer has to do with genes.

Even though both Jordans had strong muscles and excellent coordination, only one had the right gene mix for exceptional height. In high school, Larry was only 170 cm (5 ft. 7 in.) while his younger brother towered above him — and everyone else in the family. Eventually, Michael reached a height of 198 cm (6 ft. 6 in.).

With the help of his genes and plenty of hard work, Michael Jordan scored a record-breaking 10 000 points in the NBA and won the Most Valuable Player award six times.

8

The Family Shuffle

Children in one family differ from one another because humans—like pea plants, spiders, elephants and many other living things—reproduce sexually. This means half a baby's genes come from her mother and half from her father. (The baby's parents each donate a mixed set of genes they inherited from their parents.)

The mother's genes are carried in an egg cell; the father's in a sperm cell. When egg and sperm cells—also called sex cells—combine, the result is a well-shuffled combination of genes.

Dimples run in Vanessa's family. But not every family member has them. From looking at Vanessa's family tree, can you tell whether dimples are a dominant or recessive trait?

(See answer on page 39.)

Journey to Your Genes

You can see the effects of your genes by looking in the mirror. But where are your genes located in your body? To find out, imagine boarding a microscopic space probe. Your mission? To find your genes.

Zoom into the skin on your big toe. You discover that the skin tissue is divided into tiny compartments called cells. Your whole body is made of cells.

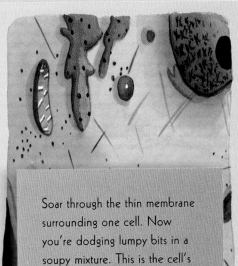

Soar through the thin membrane surrounding one cell. Now you're dodging lumpy bits in a soupy mixture. This is the cell's cytoplasm (say SITE-oh-plaz-um).

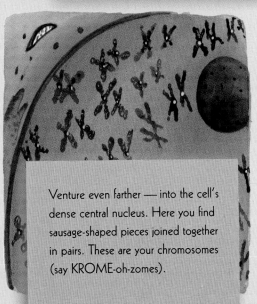

Venture even farther — into the cell's dense central nucleus. Here you find sausage-shaped pieces joined together in pairs. These are your chromosomes (say KROME-oh-zomes).

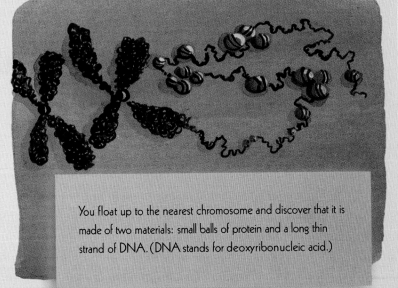

You float up to the nearest chromosome and discover that it is made of two materials: small balls of protein and a long thin strand of DNA. (DNA stands for deoxyribonucleic acid.)

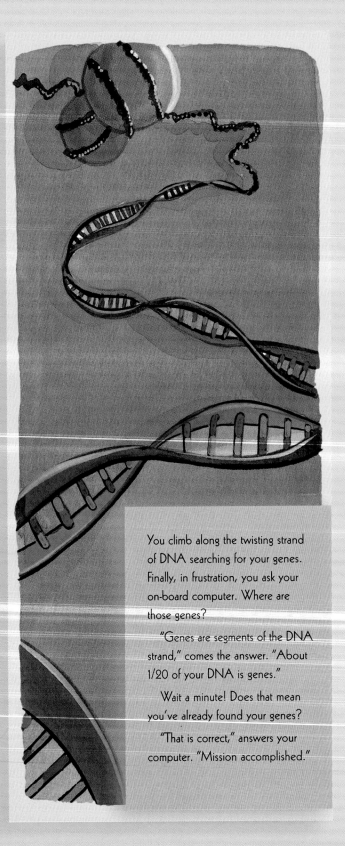

- Each cell in your body is much smaller than the period at the end of this sentence.

- You have 23 pairs of chromosomes in nearly every cell. One chromosome of each pair is from your father, one is from your mother.

Dad + Mom

- Only about 1/20 of your DNA forms genes. What does the rest of it do? Some of the DNA turns genes on and off. But scientists aren't sure about the rest, so they sometimes call it "junk" DNA.

You climb along the twisting strand of DNA searching for your genes. Finally, in frustration, you ask your on-board computer. Where are those genes?

"Genes are segments of the DNA strand," comes the answer. "About 1/20 of your DNA is genes."

Wait a minute! Does that mean you've already found your genes?

"That is correct," answers your computer. "Mission accomplished."

The Big Picture

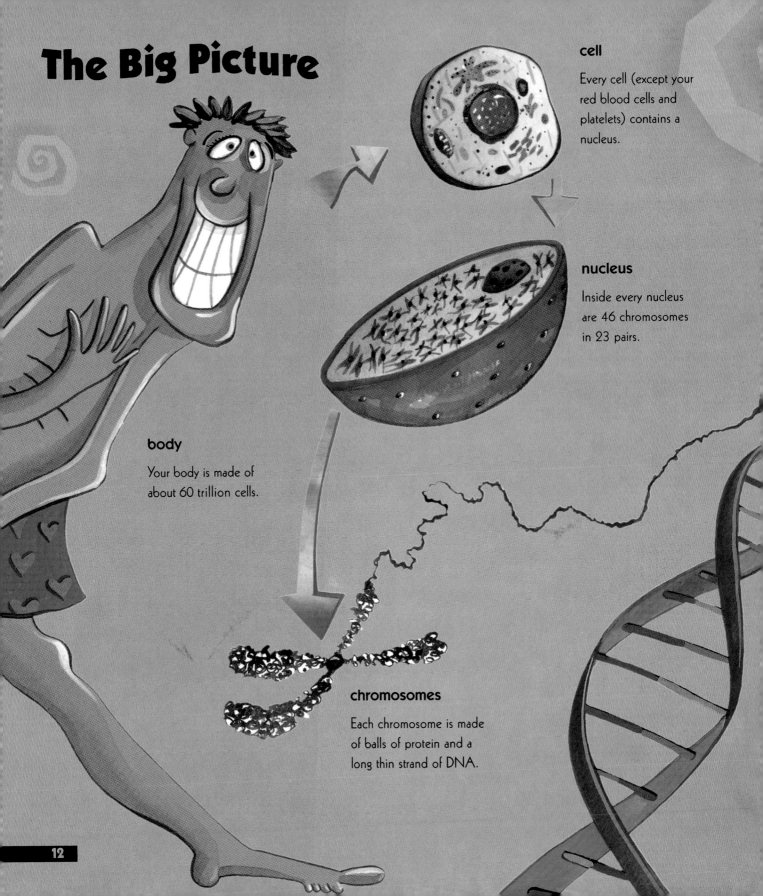

cell

Every cell (except your red blood cells and platelets) contains a nucleus.

nucleus

Inside every nucleus are 46 chromosomes in 23 pairs.

body

Your body is made of about 60 trillion cells.

chromosomes

Each chromosome is made of balls of protein and a long thin strand of DNA.

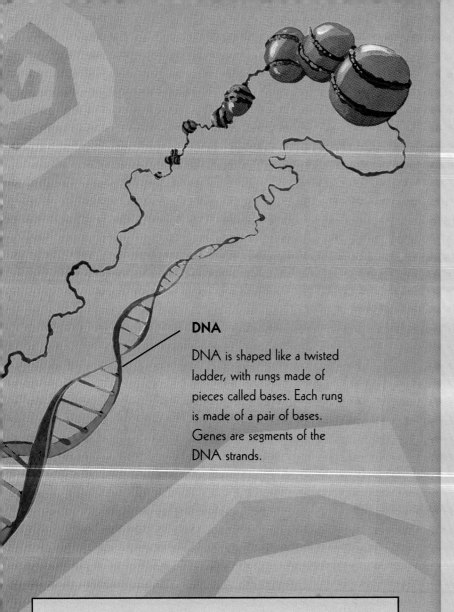

DNA

DNA is shaped like a twisted ladder, with rungs made of pieces called bases. Each rung is made of a pair of bases. Genes are segments of the DNA strands.

The DNA Code

Genes tell cells what to do. How? They use a code. The code has only four "letters"—A, T, C and G. These stand for the four bases— adenine, thymine, cytosine and guanine. When bases pair up to form rungs on the DNA ladder, adenine always connects with thymine. Cytosine always joins guanine. Through the order of the bases, the gene gives coded instructions to the cell.

You Try It

Every living thing is made of one or more cells. You can see cells by looking at onion skin under a microscope. Carefully peel off a bit of the thin white layer under the dry outer skin of a cooking onion. Place your sample on a slide and look at it using a magnification of 50 to 100 times. Plant cells, such as those of the onion, are surrounded by a cell wall. You can see onion cell walls more clearly by staining your slide with a drop of iodine. Your cells, and those of other animals, do not have walls. Instead, they have thin membranes that hold the cell together and control the flow of nutrients in and out of the cell.

Express Yourself

Your cells can be compared to the musicians in a symphony orchestra. Just as a musician follows a written musical score, a cell follows the instructions coded in your genes. And, in the same way musicians play different pieces of music at different concerts, your cells "play" different genes at different times. When you cut your finger, for instance, cells in the injured area use certain genes to direct the building of new skin tissue. Before long, the cut heals over. As you exercise, some of the genes in your leg cells provide the coded plans for new muscle fibers.

When a cell is using a gene, scientists say that gene is being "expressed." When the right genes are expressed at the right times, your body works in healthy harmony.

Genes on the Job

Your genes are like the blueprints for building a fancy house. While blueprints show a contractor where to place walls, floors and windows, genes hold the design plans for skin, muscle, bones and all the rest of you.

Each gene tells your body how to make one particular protein. Proteins, in turn, command the day-to-day functioning of your cells. Some proteins build and repair body parts, such as skin, muscles and bones, while others control all your life processes, including digestion, breathing and movement.

- Your body contains over 50 000 different proteins. Each has a special function needed for good health.

- While most genes direct normal body functioning, some have odd effects. Scientists have found a gene that makes people grow thick, furry hair all over their bodies and faces. Its nickname? The werewolf gene.

- Many human features depend on a group of genes working together. These gene groups influence things such as weight, skin and hair color.

Copycat Cells

Your body makes new cells all the time to replace worn-out ones, repair injuries and help you grow. Where do new cells come from? They're created when existing cells divide into two.

Each new cell must have a complete copy of your genes. To make sure this happens, cells go through a process called mitosis.

1. Each chromosome makes an exact replica of itself.

2. The double chromosomes line up in the center of the cell.
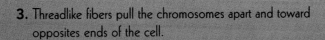

3. Threadlike fibers pull the chromosomes apart and toward opposites ends of the cell.

4. The original cell splits in two.

5. The two "daughter" cells are identical to their "parent" cell. Each holds an exact copy of your DNA.

DNA Sleuths

"We've found the secret of life!" Francis Crick proclaimed to the crowd at the Eagle pub in Cambridge, England, on February 28, 1953. He and James Watson had been working for several months to puzzle out the basic structure of DNA, the substance that forms the genes of every living thing on Earth.

Watson and Crick had several clues about DNA. Other scientists had already figured out that it was made of pieces called bases, sugars and phosphates. But no one knew the exact shape of DNA or how it worked. Watson and Crick hoped to solve the mystery by building a model. They ordered sections of metal cut to the same shapes as the bases, sugars and phosphates and began to try out different arrangements.

For several months, Watson and Crick struggled to fit the metal pieces together. It was like trying to build a huge jigsaw puzzle with no picture to guide you. Nothing seemed to connect properly. Meanwhile, they heard that other scientists were also working on the DNA puzzle. Who would be first to solve it?

Finally, Watson and Crick made a model shaped like a twisted ladder. The phosphates and sugars formed the ladder's sides, while the bases formed the rungs. The new model fit together perfectly. Watson and Crick felt their new model was so beautiful, it had to be true. They called its spiraling shape a "double helix."

Once the basic structure of DNA was known, scientists around the world began figuring out how it works. In 1962, Watson and Crick received the Nobel Prize for their part in revealing the "secret of life."

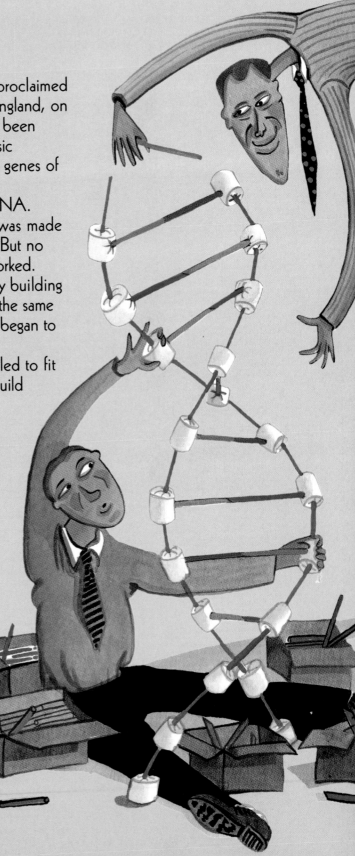

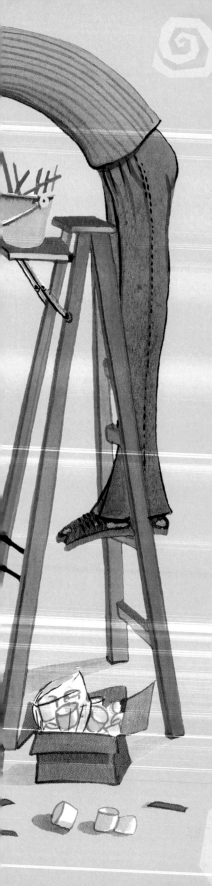

- The DNA in one human cell is so tightly coiled that it would stretch to 1 m (3 ft.) if pulled out straight.

- Laid end to end, the strands of DNA in all your cells would stretch to the Sun and back about 400 times.

- Some fish and algae have more DNA in their cells than humans.

You Try It

Use a pair of identical Slinky toys to make a simple model of DNA. Hold one Slinky in each hand. Let the Slinkys stretch down to the floor and then move them together so that their coils intertwine. The double set of spirals you've created has the same shape as DNA's double helix.

Stamping out Crime

Unless you're an identical twin or identical triplet, no one else in the world has DNA exactly like yours. Each person's DNA is unique. Because of this, DNA "prints" — obtained from tiny bits of hair, skin, blood or other body tissues — can help police solve crimes. In 1996, a DNA print helped end one of the longest criminal searches of all time, with a piece of evidence too small to be seen.

For 18 years, investigators in the United States had been searching for a man they called the Unabomber. He had mailed a series of parcel bombs that killed 3 people and injured 29 others. In 1995, investigators finally got a lead. The Unabomber sent a long letter to newspapers demanding that they print his political ideas — or more bombs would follow. The papers reluctantly printed the strange article. A few months later, David Kaczynski contacted police to say the article sounded terribly similar to letters he had received from his brother, Ted.

David led the investigators to Ted's cabin in an isolated part of Montana. There they found many pieces of evidence, including materials for making bombs and copies of the political article. Meanwhile, another crucial piece of evidence was being uncovered.

A genetic lab analyzed the DNA from saliva on stamps the Unabomber had licked when he mailed his letters to the newspapers. And they analyzed Ted Kaczynski's saliva on stamps and envelopes mailed to his brother. The DNA from both samples matched. Without a doubt, Ted Kaczynski was the Unabomber.

In 1998, Kaczynski was sentenced to life imprisonment. With the help of a few drops of spit, the case of the Unabomber was finally closed.

How It Works

To make a DNA print, a lab technician extracts DNA from a person's hair, skin, blood or other tissues. The DNA is then mixed with enzymes that break it apart. The pieces are placed in a tray and an electric current moves them through a gel. Larger fragments move more slowly than smaller, lighter ones, so the sample is sorted by length and weight. The result is "printed," revealing a pattern of dark bars, much like a bar code. DNA samples from the same person have the same pattern of bars. And each person's pattern is different.

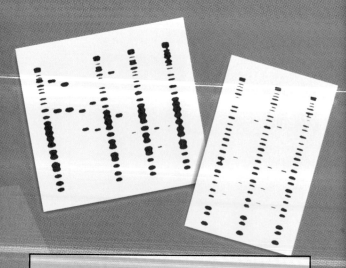

- **Some famous people use a DNA pen to make sure no one forges their signatures. The ink in the pen is mixed with the owner's saliva for a truly personal signature.**

"I Am Anastasia"

On July 16, 1918, Czar Nicholas II of Russia and his family were shot by revolutionaries. Rumors arose that the Czar's youngest daughter, Anastasia, had survived.

Two years later, on a cold February night, a young woman jumped off a bridge in Berlin, Germany. She told her rescuers she was the Grand Duchess Anastasia. Over the following years, she won many supporters, but there was no way to prove her claim. She died in 1984.

Seven years later, DNA from her hair was compared with DNA samples from relatives of the Czar. The woman was not Anastasia. The mystery of the real Anastasia continues.

Gene Error!

Robert Wadlow always wanted to fit in. But at 272 cm (8 ft. 11 in.) tall, it was hard for him to pass unnoticed. Wadlow is on record as the world's tallest man. Although he was a normal size when he was born in Alton, Illinois, in 1918, he soon started to grow — and grow. By the time he was eight, the gentle giant was taller than his father, over 2 m (6 ft.) tall. When he joined Boy Scouts at age 13, he had to duck through doorways. By 20, Wadlow was working for Ringling Brothers circus and for a company making extra-large shoes. His own were size 37.

Wadlow grew so tall because his pituitary gland produced too much growth hormone. He had a disorder called acromegaly. During Wadlow's lifetime, the disease was poorly understood. Now scientists are learning that most cases of acromegaly are caused by an error, or "mutation," in a gene that affects the pituitary gland. (The pituitary gland regulates the production of growth hormone.) A mutation in a gene can mean the gene does not provide correct instructions to the pituitary gland and too much growth hormone is produced.

Today, a person with acromegaly can be treated with surgery and drugs, but Wadlow wasn't so lucky. When he was 22 years old, his ankle became infected from the constant rubbing of a brace he needed for support. Within ten days, he died. Doctors reported that up until his death, Robert Wadlow was still growing.

Mutations

Gene mutations, like the one that caused Wadlow to grow out of control, can scramble messages to the body, causing diseases.

Mutations often happen when cells are dividing and their genes are copying themselves. Instead of being an identical copy, a mutated gene might be missing a chunk or have a piece in the wrong order.

normal DNA

broken DNA

Mutations can be inherited — passed down from parents to children in their genes. Or they can occur during a person's lifetime, as in Robert Wadlow's case. These mutations are caused by stresses on the body, such as toxic chemicals, radiation and even sunlight.

- Lucia Zarate is said to be the lightest person who ever lived. As an adult woman in the late 1890s, she weighed less than most newborn babies — about 2.3 kg (5 lbs.). Her full height was only 50 cm (20 in.). Zarate's tininess was probably caused by a mutation in one of her genes.

Skin cancer happens when sunlight causes mutations in a skin cell's genes. The mutated cell grows and divides out of control, producing a cancerous patch called a melanoma. Doctors warn that a severe sunburn in childhood can double a person's chances of getting skin cancer later in life. So protect your genes — and yourself. Avoid direct midday sun. Wear protective clothes and hats. And use sunscreen.

Earthbound Space Suit

On April 19, 1999, six-year-old Mikie Walker played in the sunlight for the first time in his life. Mikie has a genetic disease called porphyria that makes his skin so sensitive to sunlight that he can go outdoors only at night. Daylight causes his skin to blister, peel and break out in sores that won't heal.

Mikie's life changed when NASA designers used space technology to build a suit for kids like him. Wearing his "space suit," which covers him from head to toe, Mikie can roll in the grass and build sand castles on the beach, without worrying about the sun. An astronaut exploring the Moon couldn't be happier.

Protein Power

Mikie has porphyria because his liver doesn't make enough of one type of protein. Without this protein, light-sensitive pigments build up in his skin, causing sores and blisters. Why is Mikie missing this protein? Because a mutation in one of his genes gives his liver cells the wrong instructions.

A faulty gene may produce too much, too little or the wrong type of protein. When that happens, the human owner of the gene may get sick.

- People with porphyria sometimes develop reddish-tinged urine. Early stories of vampires and werewolves may have been based on misunderstanding of this rare genetic disease.

Good Mutations

Many gene mutations are bad news — they can cause illness and threaten a creature's survival. But every once in a while, a mutation produces a useful trait. If the new trait improves its owner's ability to survive, the mutated gene will be passed on to future generations. Less helpful traits disappear — their owners often die before passing along the gene. This process is known as "natural selection."

Scientists in Britain studied natural selection in moths. Some moths had a mutation that made their wing color slightly darker than normal. For moths that lived in a big city where pollution had darkened the buildings, the new dark wing color was a benefit. It helped them escape the notice of hungry birds. So the "dark-wing" trait was passed on to their offspring, who passed it to their offspring in turn. Over time, more dark moths survived and reproduced than regular, light-winged moths. Eventually, nearly every moth in the city had dark wings. Through mutation and natural selection, the moths had adapted to their environment.

- Similar genes in different species show that all living things evolved from a common ancestor.

- Chimpanzees are our closest relatives. Human and chimp DNA is 98 percent the same.

Awesome Adaptations

Over millions and millions of years, plants and animals have gradually changed through mutation and natural selection. They have become adapted to different environments all over the world. In the frozen north, white fur helps Arctic hares hide from predators. Out in the ocean, thick layers of blubber keep whales warm. Eagles soaring overhead have keen eyesight to spot their prey.

Gene mutations and natural selection have produced an incredible variety of life on Earth. Mutations have helped create zebras, butterflies, sunflowers, giant squids, redwood trees, pygmy shrews and all the other living things on Earth. These processes have even managed to produce the species known as homo sapiens — and that includes you!

You Try It

You can see natural selection at work with the help of a few energetic friends and some colored yarn. Choose six different colors of yarn. Include dull green, brown or gray as well as bright red, orange or yellow pieces. Make 20 pieces of each color. Each piece should be about 8 cm (3 in.) long. Sprinkle the yarn "worms" all over your backyard. Then invite your friends over and tell them they are the birds. Give them one minute to run around collecting as many worms as they can. The "bird" who gets the most worms is the winner.

What do you notice about the worms they've collected? Which worms are still on the grass? In nature, these better-adapted worms would survive longer and have more offspring. (Clean up by having another worm collection.)

Finding Faulty Genes

As a boy growing up in Hong Kong, Dr. Lap-Chee Tsui (pronounced "Choy") loved peering into ponds and scooping up tadpoles. These days, he spends his time poking and peering into human chromosome 7. His goal? To catch the genes that cause many serious diseases.

In 1982, Dr. Tsui began searching for the genetic mutation that causes cystic fibrosis. He knew that children born with this inherited disease often die before they are 25. Their bodies produce mucous so thick that sometimes they can't breathe.

Dr. Tsui and his colleagues set to work in their crowded lab at the Hospital for Sick Children in Toronto. Surrounded by test tubes, microscopes and computers, they tested the blood of children with cystic fibrosis. DNA from each child was compared with the DNA of healthy individuals. Dr. Tsui knew there had to be a difference somewhere.

Gene Hunting

For seven years, the search went on. Dr. Tsui's team collaborated with research groups led by Dr. John Riordan and Dr. Francis Collins. A few times, the scientists thought they had found the gene that had the mutation. But each time they rechecked their data, they were disappointed. Then, on May 9, 1989, they found a mutation in a gene on chromosome 7. The mutated gene was missing the DNA code for just one amino acid in one protein. Dr. Tsui was cautious. Could this be the difference they were looking for?

Over the next five months, the researchers checked and rechecked their findings. Every test confirmed the results. With growing excitement, the scientists realized that their search had been successful. In September 1989, Drs. Tsui, Riordan and Collins announced that the genetic mutation for cystic fibrosis had been found.

Since 1989, Dr. Tsui and other scientists have been working hard to study chromosome 7, the site of the cystic fibrosis gene and several others they suspect may cause serious diseases. Dr. Tsui hopes that learning more about how genes work will lead to treatments for children whose lives are threatened by faulty genes.

Mapping Our Genes

On June 26, 2000, scientists announced a major accomplishment. After ten years of hard work, they had succeeded in mapping the human genome.

The new map shows the order of bases — A, T, C and G — in our DNA code, but leaves many questions unanswered. Which parts of the sequence form genes? How many genes do humans have? And how, exactly, do those genes work? With the genome map as a guide, scientists are exploring these questions. Their dramatic discoveries have already begun to transform how doctors treat diseases.

You can find out the latest developments on the Human Genome Project at:

www.ornl.gov/TechResources/Human_Genome/

Fixing Faulty Genes

In 1990, four-year-old Ashanti DeSilva was a very sick girl. A faulty gene inherited from both her parents made Ashanti's body incapable of fighting off even a small infection. Common germs were deadly, so Ashanti's parents kept her in isolation in their home.

Fearing that Ashanti might die, her doctors made a drastic proposal. They wanted to give the little girl the gene she was missing. The operation would be experimental, but Ashanti's worried parents gave their consent.

On September 14, 1990, doctors removed some of Ashanti's white blood cells, loaded them with a virus carrying the healthy gene and injected them back into their small patient. Ashanti had just become the first person in the world to receive gene therapy.

Over the next few months and years, Ashanti's health improved. She's now a teenager who enjoys riding her bike and shooting baskets with her friends. Ashanti still takes medicine for her condition, but doctors feel her good health is mainly due to gene therapy. Says Ashanti's dad: "It's a miracle."

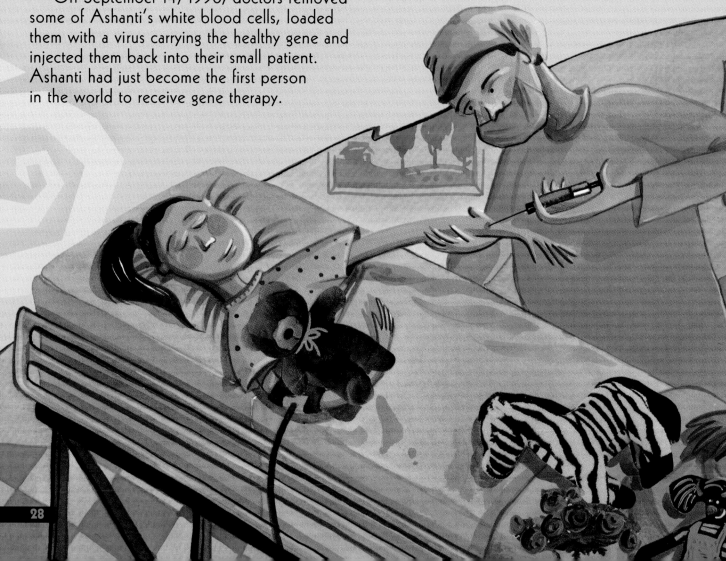

A Tough Challenge

Scientists have found many ways to insert healthy genes into sick people. But this type of gene therapy isn't always successful. The introduced genes don't always function as they should. Now, instead of trying to add genes directly to cells, many scientists are working on ways to use genes indirectly. One way is to insert them into bacteria. The genetically changed bacteria produce human proteins that doctors can use as medicines.

- Scientists use genetic engineering to change the genes of living things. They can cut up and recombine pieces of DNA to fix or replace faulty genes, or to add new genes to an existing genome.

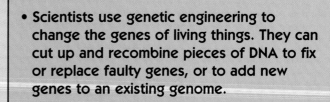

- Researchers in Wisconsin have designed a "gene gun" that fires microscopic gold bullets coated with genes into the skin of mice. The gene-coated bullets shrink tumors in mice and are being studied for use in humans.

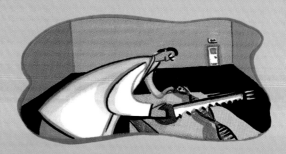

- A Canadian biotechnology company has developed an artificial chromosome. Injected into a mouse, the chromosome carries genes that are passed on to the mouse's offspring. In the future, artificial chromosomes may be used to deliver gene therapy to humans.

The Power of Pigs

Stubborn people are called pig-headed, but have you ever heard of someone being pig-hearted?

Researchers at the Mayo Clinic and other institutions are working on the possibility of using pig parts to replace failing hearts, lungs, livers and kidneys in people. Pig organs are about the same size as human organs. While some people object, many feel that it's okay to use pigs for organ donation as well as for food. The trouble is, pig organs are quickly rejected by human bodies. The human immune system produces proteins called antibodies that recognize foreign cells and try to get rid of them. This is useful when you're battling a cold virus, but not helpful when you want to accept a new organ.

To transplant pig organs successfully, scientists are working on techniques for introducing human DNA into pigs. This DNA includes the gene for making a protein that disguises pig tissues. If the human body doesn't recognize the pig organ as being foreign, it may allow it to function successfully — and extend a person's life.

Tapping into Pig Potential

Pig—human organ transplants are in the future, but some work with pigs is already saving lives.

People with a disease called hemophilia can easily bleed to death because their bodies don't make a blood-clotting protein called factor VIII. But factor VIII is difficult and costly to produce in the lab. To solve this problem, researchers have injected female pigs with the human gene for making factor VIII. The pigs produce the clotting factor in their milk, where it can easily be collected. Scientists estimate that a few hundred sows could supply all the factor VIII needed for every hemophiliac in the world.

Cloning, Cloning

Though she looked like any other cute woolly lamb, Dolly was world famous. Her birth in February 1997 was front-page news, thrilling some people and shocking others. But why all the fuss? Because Dolly, an ordinary-looking lamb, was a clone — an exact genetic copy of another sheep. It was the first time a mammal had ever been cloned from an adult, and it made people wonder if human cloning could be far behind.

Dolly was cloned by scientists who took a cell from one sheep and stimulated it to divide and develop into a brand-new animal. (All that was needed was a single cell, because each cell contains the entire genetic instructions for new life.)

The BAAAA Heard Round the World

Dolly's birth made many people realize that human cloning might be possible in the near future. Some think this would be good because it would give childless couples a chance to have a baby. Many others think human cloning would be much too risky. They point out that animal embryos often die during cloning experiments and that cloned animals are sometimes unhealthy.

Many people feel strongly that, even if cloning becomes a safe procedure for animals, it should never be done with humans. They worry that cloned children won't be treated as unique individuals, or that adults will decide to make copies of themselves for selfish reasons.

Some countries have banned research into human cloning. With so many opinions — and constant advances in cloning technologies — the debate is sure to continue.

Dinos? Doubt it. Mammoths? Maybe!

- Identical twins are sometimes called clones because they have exactly the same genes.

- Whiptail lizards in the southern United States lay eggs without mating. All their offspring are copies — or clones — of their mothers.

In the movie **Jurassic Park**, a dinosaur was cloned from a drop of blood inside a prehistoric mosquito. Could dinosaur cloning really happen? Probably not. For one thing, DNA would be destroyed over such a long stretch of time. Also, cloned embryos need a womb to grow in. What modern animal could give birth to a brontosaurus or T-rex?

In 1999, an entire 20 300-year-old mammoth was found frozen in the ice in Siberia. Scientists collected its DNA for possible cloning. They think a modern female elephant might be able to give birth to this long-extinct mammal.

Cloning Plus: Beyond Dolly

Dolly the sheep was the world's first cloned mammal. But she was soon joined by others. In 1998, researchers in Hawaii cloned several generations of identical mice. In 1999, scientists in Texas cloned a calf from an adult bull. (The adult's name was Chance. His cloned offspring? Second Chance, of course.) And in March 2000, the town of Blacksburg, Virginia, became known as the "cloned pig capital of the world" when scientists there succeeded in producing five cloned piglets.

Why do people want to make clones of animals? Mainly because animal breeders are always looking for ways to improve their livestock. By cloning an especially healthy animal, they hope to preserve its genetic strengths. But scientists and doctors also use cloned mammals and insects to study genetic mutations and human diseases, such as arthritis and cancer.

- In 1998, an American couple gave a Texas university $3.6 million to clone their dog Missy. The cloning attempt is called the Missyplicity Project.

Custom-Made Body Parts

Cloning doesn't always mean reproducing a whole plant or animal. Single cells can also be cloned to make tissues — the fabric of lungs, livers, hearts and skin.

By placing basic human cells called "stem cells" in the right conditions, scientists stimulate them to grow into various types of body tissue. Doctors have already used sheets of cloned skin tissue to replace the damaged skin of burn victims. Some researchers are experimenting with adding cloned tissue to artificial body parts, such as heart valves.

In the future, scientists might be able to clone new body parts from a patient's own cells. These "custom-made" organs could save many lives.

You look familiar

You Try It

Cloning is common in the plant world. For example, strawberry plants reproduce by sending out "runners"— long branches that sprout clones of the original plant. You can do some simple cloning by cutting a leaf from a begonia or coleus plant, placing it in potting soil and starting a new houseplant. Your new cloned plant will have exactly the same genes as its parent.

Perfect Babies ...

Scientists have made incredible advances in understanding our genes. This growing knowledge opens exciting new possibilities — and new fears.

Supporters of genetic research are optimistic about the future. Some feel that in just a few years, all new parents will receive a printout of their baby's DNA. Doctors will analyze the DNA for disease-causing mutations and use gene therapy to treat serious problems. Schools might use the child's genetic profile to identify and overcome learning difficulties. As the child grows up, she could use her DNA print to track down allergies, choose medications or order a custom-made replacement for a faulty heart or lung. With a well-maintained set of genes, she might live healthily to 120 or more.

··· or Perfect Problems?

Others worry that our new genetic knowledge brings more problems than solutions. They fear that parents-to-be may soon be able to choose or change their unborn baby's genes. Doing this could have unexpected results. For example, removing a gene for sickle-cell anemia also removes resistance to malaria. Picking a child's looks could also lead to problems. What if tall, dark-haired children are the popular choice? Will short blondes be discriminated against?

Some people worry that a person's genetic information will not be kept private. Insurance companies might refuse to insure people whose DNA shows a high risk for cancer or heart attack. Employers might not hire someone who appears to have a genetic tendency to alcoholism or mental illness.

To make sure genetic testing and therapy are used fairly, governments must pass new laws. And citizens need to inform themselves about these issues. By learning about genes and cloning, you'll be able to make wise decisions.

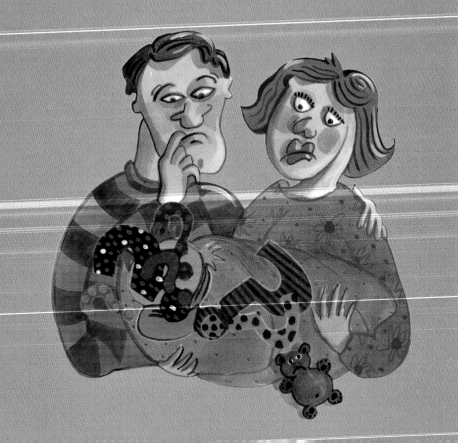

You Try It

New genetic techniques will produce many dilemmas. Here's one scenario to discuss with your family and friends.

A teenage boy's DNA test shows that he will probably develop Alzeimher's disease when he is in his 60s or 70s. Today there is no cure for this devastating disease, which robs people of their memories and thinking skills. Should the boy's parents tell him about the test results? How might this knowledge affect his outlook on life?

Into the Future

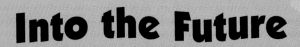

The 21st century has been called "the century of the genome." Advances happen so quickly that even genetic scientists are surprised by the latest news. By the time you read this book, many changes will have occurred. Here are some predictions. Listen to the news. Have any of these events already happened?

- Pig organs are implanted in people.
- Cystic fibrosis is cured with gene therapy.
- A person is cloned.
- Parents choose their child's genes.
- Unborn babies receive gene injections to protect them from diseases.
- Human organs are grown to order.
- Through genetic engineering, scientists extend the average human life span to 120 years or more.

Glossary

Cells: tiny compartments in living things. Bacteria are one-celled organisms. Your body has about 60 trillion cells.

Chromosomes: strands of DNA. Most of the cells in your body contain 23 pairs of chromosomes.

Clones: organisms with identical genes

Cloning: reproducing an organism with genes from just one parent

DNA (deoxyribonucleic acid): the material from which genes are made

Enzymes: proteins that control chemical reactions in cells

Evolution: changes in living things over long stretches of time

Genes: the basic units of heredity. Genes, which are passed from parents to children, influence physical traits and carry instructions for cells.

Genetic: related to genes

Genome: all the DNA in a cell

Mutation: a change in a gene

Natural selection: the process in which a trait becomes more common because it helps organisms survive

Nucleus: central part of a cell containing the chromosomes

Proteins: complex substances that form body parts and regulate body functions. Your body contains about 50 000 different proteins.

Trait: a characteristic that can be observed

Answer
You Try It, page 9:

Dimples are dominant. Think about it this way. Vanessa has no dimples. Her parents must have given her some no-dimple genes. But both Mom and Dad have dimples, so they must be carrying dimple genes as well. Because the parents' mixed genes produce dimples and not smooth cheeks in all of their children except Vanessa, we know the dimple gene is dominant.

Index